The Ego and the Id
&
Caesar and Me

An Introduction to Sigmund Freud's
Text Through The Twilight Zone

Psymedia.org Books

Matthew Tyler Giobbi, Ph.D.

CONTENTS

INTRODUCTION

Our earliest years form the foundation of not only what we think about, but more importantly, how we think. It is evident that how we think is shaped by the culture from which we emerge and the unique situations that we experience. William James likened our minds to clay on the potter's wheel; each of us uniquely formed by the pressures of the hands of culture and experience. The television media environment of the 1940s through today provides a unique ecology for understanding how we think, feel, and interact with the world.

As a child I was fascinated by the television programs that my parents' generation came of age with. In particular, I was captivated by Rod Serling's *Twilight Zone* from the 1950s and the 1960s. My father, after returning home from working the night shift at a local steel mill, would record the 1980s re-broadcasts of the show which appeared on WPIX 11 from New York City. The next day I would absorb the previous night's program, waiting for the trademark Serling twist that would come at the end—the kick that brought home the message; things aren't what they appear to be.

I started reading philosophy when I was 15 years old. A high school teacher named Terry Male had turned me on to Plato's *Parable of the Cave*—my first encounter with thinking about thinking. The themes of the cave came comfortably, I felt as if I was reading about something that I had taken for granted, namely that appearances can be different from reality. I recall being aware that the philosophy I was reading was very similar to the reruns my father had recorded for me years earlier. It turns out that I am not alone in this; many of the thinkers I meet who were born in the 1970s were influenced by Serling's *Twilight Zone*.

Throughout graduate school I would entertain myself by finding an episode (there are 156 of them) that illustrated a theoretical concept that I was studying. Some of the episodes are better than others, and not all were written by Rod Serling. What did become apparent to me was that the series was not merely about the supernatural, space aliens, and other dimensions—it was in fact a rich commentary on existential philosophy and humanism.

Rod Serling cut his writing teeth at Antioch College, in Ohio. Awarded a Purple Heart and a Bronze Star for serving in combat in World War II, Serling attended Antioch as an English major on the G.I. Bill. During college Serling converted from Judaism to Unitarianism; philosophical traces of which can be found in his writing.

2

While in college Serling submitted radio drama scripts with mixed success. Although he received over 40 rejection letters, he did manage to sell some of his work to popular radio programs. In 1950 Serling began writing for television. Adapting his radio scripts for television, many of which had to do with the soldier's struggle during war and after. He managed to shop his scripts to some of the most popular live drama programs of the golden age, including *Kraft Television Theater* and *Hallmark Hall of Fame*. Serling and his wife moved to New York City in 1954 where he would become influenced by the Beat writers and thinkers. In 1955 his 72nd script was produced by *Kraft Television Theater*, a script that would change his life. The drama was called *Patterns*. Serling followed up Patterns in 1956 with a knockout script that won him a Peabody Award and an Emmy called *Requiem for a Heavyweight*.

In 1958 Serling took on the problem of American racism and bigotry in a *Playhouse 90* teledrama called *A Town Has Turned to Dust*. The controversial drama met with considerable sponsor and executive censorship, which Serling successfully fought for broadcast. However, the experience brought corporate censorship to the forefront of Serling's concerns. He endeavored to create a program that would address civil rights issues, existentialism, and the residue of McCarthyism. Serling sought to write popular television dramas that provoked audiences to think, rather than to be merely entertained.

In *The Time Element* (1958), Serling premiered what would become his trademark psychological teledrama. He had proposed the script for a new series he called *Twilight Zone*, but instead it was presented on *The Westinghouse Desilu Playhouse*, introduced by Desi Arnaz. Not unlike Kurt Vonnegut's *Slaughterhouse Five* (1969), *The Time Element* deals with the psychological consequences of war, a theme that would recur in *Twilight Zone*.

In *Twilight Zone* we find Serling addressing the issues of death, mortality, choice, and existence that are at the heart of the human experience. Cloaked beneath the facade of space aliens, supernatural forces, or science fiction we find the weighty issues of postwar America, issues of civil rights, Red Scare McCarthyism, and the question of technology in the modern world. What Serling managed to do in *Twilight Zone* was to introduce the conversation of the postmodern condition into the living rooms of Americans who might otherwise be silent about the social conditions that their society was facing.

To the typical adolescent or adult of the 1950s and 1960s *Twilight Zone* was fantasy, Sci-Fi thriller, or purely a half-hour horror show. But for the close reader of the television text we find Serling addressing something much deeper than our fear of the outer limits; he was introducing a generation of children into the world of continental philosophy, existentialism, and Critical Theory. Serling was not telling us tales of science fiction and horror, he was showing us how to think in ways that questioned what we know as reality. The "twilight zone" is the world of the phenomenal experience, the fleshing-out of that place in which the fiction is the reality.

Peter Gay tells us that Sigmund Freud's *Das Ich und das Es* first appeared in German in 1923.[1] The English translation was made by Joan Riviere, later revised and edited by James Strachey.[2] In our reading, which is based on the Standard Edition, we keep in mind the limitations of reading any author in translation.

The Ego and the Id is often considered to be a continuation of Freud's 1920 text *Beyond the Pleasure Principle.* In what Gay calls "Freud's last major theoretical work,"[3] we find not only the description of the origins, development, and dynamics of the systems of the psyche, but also a furtherance of concepts that Freud introduced in *Beyond the Pleasure Principle.* Here we find, for the first time, the development of the super-ego, which Freud also calls the ego ideal.

I have found it useful to read Freud's *The Ego and the Id* as the second movement of a three-part work, beginning with *Beyond the Pleasure Principle* (1920)[4] and concluding with *Inhibitions, Symptoms, and Anxiety* (1926).[5] Although one can

---

[1] Peter Gay, Editor's Introduction to *The Ego and the Id,* eds. James Strachey and Peter Gay (London: Norton), xxviii.

[2] Sigmund Freud, *The Ego and the Id,* ed. James Strachey (New York: Norton, 1960).

[3] Ibid. xxix

[4] Sigmund Freud, *Beyond the Pleasure Principle,* ed. James Strachey (New York: Norton, 1961).

read *The Ego and the Id* on its own, it comes to life in the context of these other two works.

---

[5] Sigmund Freud, *Inhibitions, Symptoms, and Anxiety*, ed. James Strachey (New York: Norton, 1959).

1 CONSCIOUSNESS AND WHAT IS UNCONSCIOUS

In the opening chapter of Sigmund Freud's 1923 text, *Das Ich und das Es,* we find a statement that prefigures contemporary theories of consciousness.

> "...psycho-analysis cannot situate the essence of the psychical in consciousness, but is obliged to regard consciousness as a quality of the psychical, which may be present in addition to other qualities or may be absent."

What Freud is reiterating in this opening paragraph is the idea that consciousness is a mental process that precedes any talk of reality as such. This statement, which Freud calls "the first shibboleth of psycho-analysis," is at the center of contemporary neuroscientific theories of consciousness. The shibboleth that Freud speaks of in 1923 is the questioning of the assumptions of objectivity itself; it is a question that leads to an unraveling of the Enlightenment assumption of a subject perceiving an object.

Freud continues,

> "To most people who have been educated in philosophy the idea of anything psychical which is not also conscious is so inconceivable that it seems to them absurd and refutable simply by logic. I believe this is not only because they have never studied the relevant phenomenon of hypnosis and dreams, which—quite apart from pathological manifestations—necessitate this view." (Pg. 3)

What we find here is a critique that applies directly to any theory of mind that assumes objective reality outside of our conscious experience. We see a direct attack of objective theory that suggests that a world is independent of the mind's production of consciousness. This is central to the psychodynamic proposition of the structure of the self, which Freud fully develops for the first time in this text. It is also a critique of much of the research that continues to be taught in the social sciences, namely that objectivity is somehow parsable from subjectivity; the endeavor of positivistic empiricism. The proof of Freud's thesis is shown by examples from the dream life and hypnosis, which constitute a psychical production of reality. Cognitive neuroscience calls this top-down processing.

In the English translation (*The Ego and the Id*, 1925) we find a model that allows us to consider conscious experience of not only the world and others, but also of ourselves. But we must keep in mind that this theory is one which proposes that reality is a participatory act of the mind, one that is also found in the later writing of Wilhelm

Wundt through his concept of voluntaristic apperception.

Freud proposes four systems that interact dynamically to produce the phenomenon of the self. These four entities are all aspects of the psyche as a whole and interact dynamically (psycho-dynamic). We experience these four systems (the external world, the ego, the id, and the super-ego) as a unity, what we call our *self*.

The 1964 *Twilight Zone* episode, *Caesar and Me* provides us with an illustration of much of what is proposed by Freud in *The Ego and the Id*. Written by Adele T. Strassfield, *Caesar and Me* would be the only episode of *The Twilight Zone* to be written by a woman.

Caesar and Me is the story of a ne'er-do-well ventriloquist named Jonathan West (Jackie Cooper) who is arrested after turning to a life of crime. The story unfolds as West's ventriloquist dummy, Caesar, comes to life and talks West into committing crimes. At the end of the drama we find Caesar talking a young girl named Susan (Morgan Brittany) into murdering her aunt.

Ostensibly we have the paranormal story of a ventriloquist's doll coming to life and convincing his owner to commit self-destructive crimes. However, if we consider the characters and the story in the context of Freud's *Ego and the Id*, we find a working illustration of the dynamics of the psyche.

There are four characters, each playing a unique role in the drama: West (the ventriloquist), Caesar (the dummy), Susan (the niece of the West's landlady), and Mrs. Cudahy (West's landlady). Each of these characters correspond to one of the four systems of the psyche that Freud describes. We are told the story from West's point of view; we experience reality, as West does, as something outside of himself. However, if we view the drama as West's *projection*, that is, as each character embodying an aspect of West's psyche, we come to see that the episode is a meta-psychology of West himself. In other words, each player of the drama is a part of West; a part which is projected into a conscious awareness of reality.

Let us consider the four systems in this way. In West we find illustrated Freud's concept of Ego (Ich). Caesar is the manifestation of id (das Es). Susan embodies super-ego (Über-Ich, also called the ego ideal). Finally, Mrs. Cudahy, along with the police, and the nightclub owners, serve as West's perceptual conscious, that is, the external world that functions on the reality principle.

In the opening scene we find Jonathan West selling a family heirloom watch at a Goldstein's pawnshop. Goldstein assures a defeated West that "things will get better". As West is leaving the shop, Goldstein motions to West's ventriloquist case, offering him $25 for his dummy. "Oh no," responds West, "No thank you, no. He is not for sale."

In this opening scene it is established that West and Caesar are inseparable. Closer even than the memory of West's own grandfather (represented by his watch) West views Caesar as part of himself, something that is "not for sale".

This exchange illustrates at least two things from the

first chapter of *The Ego and the Id*. Firstly, we understand that ego and id are fused; that the id is more valuable to the ego than any material object or family tie. Secondly, we are shown an act of repression in service of the id. West transfers his family history from conscious to unconscious in the act of pawning his grandfather's watch. We are told that this repression is not permanent, that he will have thirty days to get his watch back. What we find here is the ego repressing something from conscious awareness (West's hands) to the unconscious (his watch disappears into his well-guarded unconscious—the shop keeper's storeroom).

Freud illustrates that through repression the ego transfers awareness from conscious to unconscious. We must remember that this is not something that exists outside of the psyche, conscious and unconscious are systematic states produced by the psyche. This is illustrated by the fact that we are at once watching the story of Jonathan West's psyche from the eyes of Jonathan West. In this way, the episode is a kind of meta-cognition of the experience of the self. Freud tells us:

> "There is a coherent organization of mental processes; and we call this his ego. It is to this ego that consciousness is attached; the ego controls the approaches to motility—that is, to the discharge of excitations into the external world; it is the mental agency which supervises all its own constituent processes, and which goes to sleep at night, though even then it exercises the censorship on dreams. From this ego proceed the repressions, too, by means of which it is sought to exclude certain trends in the mind not merely from consciousness but also from other forms of effectiveness and activity." (Pg. 8)

What we see here is that the ego (the "I") is the manager of all aspects of the psyche. It serves as perceptual conscious of the world and others, and the realistic pressures of those objects (functions on the reality principle), but is also partially unconscious. That is to say, the ego is somewhat hidden from itself. In Freud's words:

> "We have come upon something in the ego itself which is also unconscious, which behaves exactly like the repressed—that is, which produces powerful effects without itself being conscious and which requires special work before it can be made conscious." (Pg. 9)

Freud goes on to say that the neurosis arises from a conflict between the coherent ego and the aspect of itself that it has repressed. We find here that the act of West repressing his conscious memory of his family might be at the root of the psychic drama that is about to unfold. We must note here that Freud clearly states that the ego is partly unconscious.

2 THE EGO AND THE ID

In chapter two of *The Ego and the Id*, Freud describes the nature and dynamics of the ego and the id. In the opening sentence Freud announces a shift in his theoretical focus from repression to the ego. The question we are confronted with is: How is it possible to know the unconscious—how do we become conscious of the unconscious?

Freud makes a point to reiterate that ego is both conscious and unconscious, a quality that, in today's classroom, is often only ascribed to the super-ego. The ego is said to be the first system that is reached by the outside world. The conscious ego receives all sensations from the external world (Freud calls these sense-perceptions) and from the internal sensations and feelings. But there is one other aspect of the internal world that we must consider; namely thoughts. Freud asks, "How does a thing become preconscious? ...Through becoming connected with the presentations corresponding to it."

Thoughts are language, and Freud describes language as that which makes a thought conscious. Thoughts that do not have a word-presentation remain unconscious (Ucs.), whereas thoughts, "through becoming connected with the word-presentation corresponding to it" become preconscious. The preconscious (Pcs.) that Freud describes here is much like what cognitive psychologists today call the short-term-memory.

Freud describes that "only something that has once been a Cs. perception can become conscious, and that anything arising from within the psyche (apart from feelings) that seeks to become conscious must try to transform itself into external perceptions...by means of memory-traces." What Freud is describing here is how a thought or memory that we do not have a word to describe is projected onto the outside world (cathexis) without our conscious awareness of it. He makes a clear distinction here that a memory is something that we are consciously aware is not a perception, whereas a hallucination is a perceptual cathexis of the unconscious that we experience as something in the outside world, but is actually from our unconscious.

In *Caesar and Me* we find this interplay between conscious, preconscious, and unconscious as illustrated by the id (Caesar), the ego (West), and the super-ego (Susan) passing in and out of West's room. The door that separates the boarding house lobby from West's room is a boundary between the conscious and the unconscious—a psychic muscle that is controlled by the ego (West holds the key). We find that most of the dialogue that takes place between West, Caesar, and Susan is in West's room—it is taking place unconsciously. In fact, we will notice that West only hears Caesar while in this room, or from within Caesar's trunk.

Freud emphasizes the distinction between linguistic and iconic thinking. "Thinking in pictures," he writes, "is...only a very incomplete form of becoming conscious. In some way, too, it stands nearer to unconscious processes than does thinking in words, and it is unquestionably older than the latter both ontogenetically and phylogenetically." What Freud is telling us here is that visual thinking is more primal, both to personal history and to the history of our species.

These early, visual, memories are largely unconscious and find conscious expression through cathexis, that is, by fusing with some word-image of the conscious. In other words, what is unconscious within us finds conscious expression in our perception of reality.

James Strachey points out in a footnote (Pg. 17) that Friedrich Nietzsche used the term id (das Es) to signify "whatever in our nature is impersonal and, so to speak, subject to natural law." Freud credits his discussion of the id to George Groddeck. The remainder of chapter two describes the characteristics and dynamics of this system.

Just as we only hear Caesar speak from within West's room, the id functions unconsciously. The id speaks through cathexis, that is, though fusing thought with some external perception—usually through dreams, hallucinations, or symptoms. When West is alone in his room, he and Caesar speak within the unconscious. The fact that West and Caesar only speak in the unconscious makes it apparent that the ego also functions somewhat unconsciously. We will see that it is only when reality intrudes into the unconscious, in the final scene of the drama, that Caesar no longer speaks to West. The unconscious has been made conscious.

There is an important distinction to be made between Jonathan West speaking for Caesar, and Caesar speaking for Jonathan West. When in conscious reality, that is, outside of the room, Caesar only speaks as an agent of Jonathan West. It is not until West and Caesar (the ego and the id) are in West's room (the unconscious) that Caesar is heard speaking for himself.

In figure 1, the only figure we find in *The Ego and the Id*, Freud illustrates the following:

> "We might add, perhaps, that the ego is that part of the id which has been modified by the direct influence of the external world through the medium of the *Pcpt.-Cs.*; in a sense it is an extension of the surface-differentiation. Moreover, the ego seeks to bring the influence of the external world to bear upon the id and its tendencies, and endeavors to substitute the reality principle for the pleasure principle that reigns unrestrictedly in the id. For the ego, perception plays the part, which in the id falls to instinct. The ego represents what may be called reason and common sense, in contrast to the id, which contains the passions." (Pg. 18)

The characteristics of the ego and the id, which Freud describes here, are evident in both West and Caesar. West, in a continual state of negotiation with the demanding and desiring Caesar exemplifies the dynamic that Freud describes between the ego and the id. Freud adds:

> "The functional importance of the ego is manifested in the fact that normally control over the approaches of motility devolves upon it. Thus in its relation to the id it is like a man on horseback, who has to hold in check the superior strength of the horse; with this difference, that the rider tries to do so with his own strength while the ego uses borrowed forces. The analogy may be carried a little further. Often a rider, if he is not to be parted from his horse, is obliged to guide it where it wants to go, so in the same way the ego is in the habit of transforming the id's will into action as if it were its own." (Pg. 19)

3 THE EGO AND THE SUPER-EGO (EGO IDEAL)

Jonathan and Caesar do not make the story. The drama can only unfold when there are outside pressures, reality, which intrudes upon Jonathan and Caesar. The subject of our story is not Jonathan, but rather, Caesar. Jonathan West himself only emerges as a character from the presence of outside forces.

Freud describes how the ego emerges from the id as a result of tensions on the id from the outside world. We can see this in the newborn infant, who is little more than a bundle of biological drives with a perceptual system (the five senses). Through the intrusion of others, the infant begins to develop a sense of self; the ego. The ego emerges from the id as a circumstance of the demands from the outside world. The initial point of contact is directly between the outside world, the perceptual system, and id. From this initial contact emerges ego; a sense of self.

Susan embodies the super-ego (also called the ego ideal). Shooting poison darts, she is, from the beginning, a tormentor, tyrant, and dictator to Jonathan. We find here a resentful young girl who berates and chastises Jonathan for all of his shortcomings. "Want to bet you didn't get a job?" she taunts Jonathan. Her hostility and antagonism are the hallmarks of the authoritarian demands of the self-righteous.

These are the characteristics of the super-ego, that part of our self that repeats the demands of the overbearing, controlling parent, police, political, and social system. In Freud's description it demands, "You ought to be like this (like your father). It also comprises the prohibition: 'You may not be like this (like your father)-- that is, you may not do all that he does; some things are his prerogative" (Pg. 30). Freud continues,

> "The super-ego retains the character of the father, while the more powerful the Oedipal complex was and the more rapidly it succumbed to repression (under the influence of authority, religious teaching, schooling and reading), the stricter will be the domination of the super-ego over the ego later on--in the form of conscience or perhaps of an unconscious guilt." (Pg. 30)

But Susan is more than a mere high-minded pest. Jonathan seems hardy in his ability to brush off Susan's reproaches (in one scene he actually reprimands her). But there she is something more than a vehement child, she is a window into an aspect of Jonathan's psyche. Susan is a glimpse of West's experience of his parents and the residue of his childhood. She personifies the wellspring of reproaches that Jonathan will make against himself--the source of his depression and impotence.

Freud details how the super-ego manifests from the ego and the id through the Oedipal imbroglio that is experienced in early childhood. We find a clue to Jonathan's childhood Oedipal conflict in the first conversation he has with Caesar.

> Jonathan: "You just sit right here and relax and I'll fix us some dinner! A fella deserves something in his stomach at the end of a tough day, huh? Now, this ought to do it, I'll warm up some of that fine potato soup I made for you. And don't you worry, we're gonna get a bookin' any day now, you and me. We're gonna be headliners! Just like you and that other fella used to be...only I won't skip out on you like he did. No sir. The shame of it all. Abandoning you for some woman. No sir. It's gonna be you and me pal; together forever!"

What we find here is Jonathan having a conversation with himself. He is speaks to himself as a parent speaks to a child. What is important in this conversation is that Jonathan expresses a loss. At some point in his life someone (presumably a parent) betrayed him, "skipped out on him," as he puts it. This loss (experienced as a betrayal) exhibits the experience of the little child who, when coming to terms with the simultaneous need to be the absolute meaning of one parent's existence, and the fear of abandonment and punishment from the other parent; illustrates the Oedipal situation. Freud claims that the super-ego develops as a psychic internalization of a love object that is lost.

We can't conjecture who Jonathan's lost love object was, but we can suppose that Jonathan's impotence is somehow rooted in this early loss. Freud tells us, "...an object which was lost has been set up again inside the ego--that is, that an object-cathexis has been replaced by an identification." Freud goes on to describe how the super-ego serves as the foundation for our friendships, how we form social bonds with others based on our identification with others who share our experience of conscience (morality).

> "It is easy to show that the ego ideal answers to everything that is expected of the higher nature of man. As a substitute for a longing for the father, it contains the germ from which all religions have evolved. The self-judgment which declares the ego falls short of its ideal produces the religious sense of humility to which the believer appeals in his longing. As a child grows up, the role of father is carried on by teachers and others in authority; their injunctions and prohibitions remain powerful in the ego ideal and continue, in the form of conscience, to exercise the moral censorship. The tension between the demands of conscience and the actual performances of the ego is experienced as a sense of guilt. Social feeling rest on identifications with other people, on the basis of having the same ego-ideal." (Pg.33)

The closest hint of a social bond that Jonathan West experiences is with Mrs. Cudahy, whom we assume shares familial history similar to West's (her last name indicates that she is of the same Irish ancestry as West). This social bond is frustrated by West who, by all accounts, is not only friendless but asexual, an issue Freud takes up next.

4 THE TWO CLASSES OF INSTINCTS

Freud tells us that two impulses are predisposed at birth: a drive towards life and an drive towards death. The event of birth is something endured, not something invited. Freud claims that humans yearn to "re-establish a state of things that was disturbed by the emergence of life." Here we find Freud describing the idea of the death-drive, the opposition of Eros, the life-drive. Eros had been the lone drive in Freud's theory, a bifurcation of the desire for sexual objects and the desire for self-preservation.

We find that the life-drive and the death-drive are not merely in opposition, but are also fused and complimentary. Freud tells us that "...a special physiological process (of anabolism or catabolism) would be associated with each of the two classes of instincts; both kinds of instinct would be active in every particle of living substance..." Freud describes the death-drive as a necessary part of the organism protecting itself "against the external world," in other words it is "alloyed with" the life-drive.

An instance of this fusing can be found in the "sadistic component of the sexual instinct... and the sadism which has made itself independent as a perversion [that] would be typical of a defusion..." This fusion and defusion between the life and death instincts, Freud surmises, is not only the core of sexual sadism, but also the impulse for the "fundamental phenomenon" of ambivalence -our simultaneous feelings of desire and disgust, often experienced as the simultaneous desire to be both protected and independent -"the polarity of love and hate". Freud characterizes this:

> "There is no difficulty in finding a representative of Eros; but we must be grateful that we can find a representative of the elusive death instinct in the instinct of destruction, to which hate points the way. Now, clinical observation shows not only that love is with unexpected regularity accompanied by hate (ambivalence), and not only that in human relationships hate is frequently a forerunner of love, but also that in a number of circumstances hate changes into love and love into hate." (Pg.41)

In Jonathan West we find curiously little evidence of either a life-drive or a death-drive. His words and actions with others are empty placeholders, temporary acts that fend-off and forestall the intrusion of reality. This is most obvious when we see West auditioning for a ventriloquist job. His act is unconvincing, dispirited, and impotent. The same is true with his interactions with other objects of reality, including Mrs. Cudahy; West is repeatedly inert to his landlady's overtures of nurturing and love. We get the

23

feeling that West is somehow unable to respond to her willingness for affection. The only emotional investment we find in West is within himself.

Freud describes how the erotic libido (the sex drive) can be transformed into ego-libido (self-preservation drive), which serves to de-sexualize the libidinal energy. Freud describes this de-sexualization of the libido as a way of dealing with the loss of a love object, particularly a forbidden love object, such as the cultural restrictions of a homosexual love object-cathexis. Freud tells us,

> "By thus getting hold of the libido from the object-cathexis, setting itself up as sole love-object, and desexualizing or sublimating the libido of the id, the ego is working in opposition to the purposes of Eros and placing itself at the service of the opposing instinctual impulses." (Pg. 45)

This, of course, is illustrated by Jonathan West's narcissism. His only investment of libidinal energy is with himself, that is, with Caesar and Susan. In an attempt to deal with some object-loss in reality, West has redirected his erotic libido onto himself, which leaves nothing for the external world. Freud tells is, "The narcissism of the ego is thus a secondary one, which has been withdrawn from objects."

It is important to note that Freud does not point to homosexual object desire as the cause of this neurotic way of dealing with the world. This illustration clearly shows that it is the forbidden status of that homoerotic desire that the ego reacts to. In other words, it is the social imposition against the desire, rather than the desire itself, that results in the shift from love of the object to disgust. Freud illustrates this economic redirection of the drives with a joke. "Such behavior on the part of the unconscious reminds one of the comic story of the three village tailors, one of whom had to be hanged because the only village blacksmith had committed a capital offence."

We find Caesar, in playing the role of id, driven by the pleasure principle. His demands are life-preserving, an attempt to counterbalance the narcissistic deflation of the ego. We see that without Caesar's prodding, West would be little more than a living corpse. Freud tells us that this relationship is "illustrated in Fechner's principle of constancy... [it] governs life, which thus consists of a continuous descent towards death, it is the claims of Eros, of the sexual instincts, which in the form of instinctual needs, hold up the falling level and introduce fresh tensions." Here we can see that far from being merely destructive, Caesar is the one force that is keeping Jonathan from death.

Freud concludes the penultimate chapter of the book with a description of how the ego and id corroborate in a maintaining the life-drive. Through this description of the id's drive towards pleasure, we can understand how Caesar, far from being a mere destructive force in West, is also a life-sustaining function that keeps West alive.

"This accounts for the likeness of the condition that follows complete sexual satisfaction to dying, and for the fact that death coincides with the act of copulation in some of the loser animals. These creature die in the act of reproduction because, after Eros had been eliminated through the process of satisfaction, the death instinct has a free hand for accomplishing its purpose. Finally, as we have seen, the ego, by sublimating some of the libido for itself and its purposes, assists the id in its work of mastering the tensions." (Pg. 47)

5 THE DEPENDENT RELATIONSHIPS
OF THE EGO

Whereas much of the first four chapters of *The Ego and the Id* describe the origins, development, and nature of the systems of the psyche, this final chapter deals with the dynamics of those systems; how they act and interact.

Freud begins the final chapter by summarizing what has been explored in the previous four chapters, namely how the ego and super-ego emerge from the id as identifications with lost love objects (abandoned cathexes). Freud tells us that the development of these three systems of the psyche not only mirror the child's development through puberty and adulthood, but also preserve the conflicts (complexes) that a child experiences during those years. "As the child was once under a compulsion to obey its parents, so the ego submits to the categorical imperative of its super-ego."(Pg. 49). Freud goes on to remind us that,

> "...the super-ego is always close to the id and can act as its representative *vis-à-vis* the ego. It reaches deep down into

27

the and for that reason is farther from consciousness than the ego is." (Pg. 49)

The above passages illustrate for us the dynamic nature of the psyche, namely that there are aspects of the super-ego and the id that are unknown to the ego; private conversations that take place behind the back of the ego. It is important to recall that Freud described that the ego itself is partially unconscious and unknown to itself.

In *Caesar and Me* we find conversations between Jonathan West and Caesar only taking place in Jonathan's room. The room is private and closed off from reality--a place where conversations take place between West, Caesar, and Susan. Whereas West's conversations outside of the room are placating, superficial, and hurried, his conversations inside his room are deliberate, penetrating, and searching. West's internal dialogue, the unconscious thoughts that express the demands of the id and super-ego, is authentic, whereas the conversations he has outside of the room (conscious conversations) are calculated performances, ego defenses against the demands of reality. We also note that Susan and Caesar have conversations unknown to Jonathan, illustrating the unconscious dynamics that Freud describes, between the super-ego and the id.

Jonathan has just settled his debt with his landlady using money that he swiped from the neighborhood delicatessen. Jonathan, Mrs. Cudahy, and Susan interact in the lobby of the boardinghouse. Mrs. Cudahy is supportive and encouraging to West while Susan berates him, "Will wonders never cease... Better count it again, Auntie, see if they're real." We find here the dynamic interaction of the ego, super-ego, and reality taking place in consciousness. The id is silent, only speaking unconsciously. It is not until we enter West's room (the unconscious) that we find Caesar admonishing Jonathan:

West: A common thief. What a way to make a living.

Caesar: You couldn't make it any other way.

West: What's happened to me? A no-talent ventriloquist. Worse, a second-rate thief.

Caesar: Third-rate.

West: Starving to death. In the profession I know, paying the bills by robbing the neighborhood delicatessen.

Caesar: Well, that's show biz.

West: I guess I wasn't too bad considering it was my opening performance.

Caesar: Let me straighten you out before you start taking too many bows.

West: Oh Caesar, just let me alone, please.

Let's first consider the dynamics of the conscious interaction between West and Mrs. Cudahy. West is always placating, polite, and superficial with Mrs. Cudahy. It is as if he is *acting as one acts when one is in public*. West is performing, meeting the demands of reality by obsequiously capitulating to the social commandments of civilized society. His interaction with reality is consistently submissive and appeasing, as if to say, "pardon me for my impotence". West is almost deaf to Mrs. Cudahy's praise. Freud tells us,

"There are certain people who behave in a quite peculiar fashion during the work of analysis. When one speaks hopefully to them or expresses satisfaction with the progress of the treatment, they show signs of discontent and their condition invariably becomes worse... One becomes convinced, not only that such people cannot endure any praise or appreciation, but that they react inversely to the progress of the treatment... They exhibit what is known as a 'negative therapeutic reaction'... We are accustomed to say that the need for illness has got the upper hand in them over the desire for recovery... In the end we come to see that we are dealing with what may be called a 'moral' factor, a sense of guilt, which is finding satisfaction in the illness and refuses to give up the punishment of suffering." (Pg. 49)

Despite the fact that West is satisfying his debt, he is unable to accept praise from Mrs. Cudahy. Meanwhile, Susan is whipping him with for his sin, partly in consciousness and unconscious, she knows the true origin of West's payment, and she won't allow him to forget it. Susan is West's conscience seeping through into consciousness. It is clear that West is suffering from guilt. Freud tells us how this *unconscious guilt* functions:

"An interpretation of the normal, conscious sense of guilt (conscience) presents no difficulties; it is based on the tension between the ego and the ego ideal and is the expression of a condemnation of the ego by its critical agency. The feelings of inferiority so well known in neurotics are presumably not far removed from it... In melancholia the impression is that the super-ego has obtained a hold upon consciousness is even stronger. But here the ego ventures no objection; it admits its guilt and submits to the punishment... in melancholia the object to which the super-ego's wrath applies had been taken into the ego through identification." (Pg. 52)

We find here why West must not take compliments from Mrs. Cudahy, for he feels he deserves punishment for his guilt. This underlying guilt is latent and pervades West's entire character. The guilt is not merely over the petty crime of robbery; it is a much deeper guilt that, in fact, the guilt drives West to commit crimes. Freud tells us,

"It was a surprise to find that an increase in this *Ucs.* sense of guilt can turn people into criminals. But it is undoubtedly the fact. In many criminals, especially youthful ones, it is possible to detect a very powerful sense of guilt, which existed before the crime, and is therefore not its result but its motive. It is as if it was a relief to be able to fasten unconscious sense of guilt on to something real and immediate." (Pg. 53)

What Freud proposes is that underlying both depression (melancholia) and neurotic obsessions (Obsessive-Compulsions) is unconscious guilt. The former resulting symptom is self-reproachment, while the latter is pleading and forestalling. Each, Freud surmises, is incited by an unconscious intrusion of the death-drive. In other words, depression and obsession are both unique expressions of the ego's defense against the unconscious desire to return to the inorganic--to die. Freud warns, "The more a man controls his aggressiveness, the more intense becomes the ego ideal's inclination to aggressiveness against his ego." In other words, repressed aggression results in self-admonishment, illustrated clearly in the relationship between Susan and West.

What is it that Jonathan fears? Freud tells us, "The superior being, which turned into the ego ideal, once threatened castration and this dread of castration is probably the nucleus round which the subsequent fear of conscience has gathered; it is this dread that persists as the fear of conscience." (Pg. 60) What we find here is that we are driven not by guilt or conscience, but rather, to the unconscious fear of what conscience threatens to do to us. At a primal level it is castration, the symbolic annihilation of the self.

In the final scene of *Caesar and Me* we find the collapse of the dynamic structure of the self. The boundary between conscious and unconscious is breached as the unconscious is penetrated by the external world (reality). Two police officers enter the room and witness the breakdown of Jonathan West. An anonymous phone call has led the police to Jonathan as a suspect in a crime. Of course this anonymous call was from Susan, illustrating how the super-ego betrays the ego as symptoms, which, although anonymous by nature, can be seen by others. In response to Jonathan's monologue of confession, begging, and acceptance, Caesar is silent. The intrusion of reality marks the collapse of the ego defenses and the dynamic self. What remains is an unconscious, which is vacant of the ego; a Jonathan West his has been reduced to id and super-ego, without conscious expression.

ABOUT THE AUTHOR

Matthew Tyler Giobbi, Ph.D., is a media theorist who focuses on psychodynamic and existential-phenomenological theory. He is the founder of psymedia.org and teaches media psychology at Rutgers University at Newark, New Jersey. Giobbi is the Erich Fromm Research Associate at the European Graduate School in Switzerland.
Visit: www.psymedia.org
www.mgiobbi.com

www.ingramcontent.com/pod-product-compliance
Lightning Source LLC
Chambersburg PA
CBHW070405290526
45790CB00004B/1642